Earth: Slow Changes

Table of Contents

by Melissa McDaniel

Introduction

Pick up a rock. Does it feel hard and solid? Does it seem powerful? A rock rolling down a hill can crush things.

Now think of raindrops falling. Do they seem solid and powerful? No? Well, raindrops may not be able to crush things. But, over time, they can wear away rock.

When raindrops hit the ground, they break loose tiny bits of dirt and rock. As the raindrops move, they carry the tiny bits along with them. The bits of dirt and rock slowly wear away Earth's surface.

Wind and ice wear away the earth, too. So does sand. This wearing away is called **erosion** (ih-ROH-zhuhn). Over millions of years, erosion has shaped Earth. In this book, you'll find out how erosion has slowly changed Earth.

It's a Fact

The Appalachian Mountains once rose higher than 30,000 feet. Over millions of years, erosion wore them away. Now the highest point in the Appalachians is just 6,684 feet.

The Appalachian Mountains seem tall today, but they were much taller before erosion wore them down.

Glaciers

▲ **Glaciers cover almost all of the huge island of Greenland.**

I magine a giant chunk of ice, the kind you might see after a big snowstorm. Now think about a piece of ice as big as a mountain. What would happen if that mountain of ice started to move? It would flatten everything in its path, right?

Giant chunks of ice that move are called **glaciers**. Glaciers slide slowly down any slope. The ice in some glaciers is thousands of feet thick.

Ice History

Today glaciers cover about one-tenth of Earth. But in the past, Earth was much cooler. Then, more of Earth was covered with glaciers. These periods were ice ages.

The last great ice age ended about 10,000 years ago. Glaciers covered most of North America then.

Ice That Covers Earth

About one-tenth of Earth's land is permanently covered with ice. Can you guess which place has the most permanent ice today?

Place	Area (square miles)
Antarctica	5,250,000 (12,588,000 square kilometers)
North Polar Regions (Greenland, Northern Canada, Arctic Ocean Islands)	799,000 (2,070,000 square kilometers)
Asia	44,000 (115,000 square kilometers)
Alaska and Rocky Mountains	29,700 (76,900 square kilometers)
South America	10,200 (26,500 square kilometers)
Iceland	4,699 (12,170 square kilometers)

It's a Fact

Scientists can learn a lot about Earth's history from glaciers. Over time, the ice in a glacier builds up layer upon layer. Scientists have drilled down more than two miles through a glacier in Antarctica.

The ice at the bottom of this hole formed about 420,000 years ago. Scientists are studying the little bubbles of air trapped in the ice. These bubbles can tell them what Earth's weather and air were like back then.

Glaciers move very slowly. The average speed of a glacier is less than two feet per year. But no matter how slowly glaciers move, they change the land that they cross.

Some glaciers start to move high in the mountains. They scrape against mountain walls. They make them smooth.

Other glaciers push their way through narrow **canyons**. They turn the canyons into wide, U-shaped valleys.

▲ Ruth Glacier is on the slopes of Mount McKinley, in Denali National Park, Alaska.

The Ice Meets the Sea

When they move, many glaciers end up in the sea. When a glacier hits the ocean, huge pieces of ice break off the glacier and fall into the water. Each of these huge pieces of ice becomes an iceberg. Today, the world's largest iceberg is about as big as the state of Rhode Island! In time, it will break up and melt.

▲ Ice falls from a glacier into the sea.

▼ Some glaciers carve narrow, steep-sided inlets when they reach the ocean. These inlets are called **fjords** (fee-AWRDZ). This fjord is in Norway.

After the Ice Melts

In winter, snow and ice sometimes make potholes in roads. Well, glaciers can make potholes, too. They are called **glacial potholes**. This spinning water digs deep, narrow holes in the ground. These holes are glacial potholes.

As a glacier melts, water gets trapped under the heavy ice. As the ice pushes down on the water, the water sometimes begins to spin. The spinning water can reach speeds of 125 miles per hour.

When a glacier melts, it leaves behind all the rocks and dirt it was carrying. These big piles of rock and dirt can form rows of low hills. The hills are shaped like eggs and are called **drumlins**.

In other places, glaciers might leave behind a single huge rock. A giant rock left sitting all by itself is called an **erratic boulder**. Glaciers sometimes move boulders hundreds of miles.

It's a Fact

Long ago, glaciers moved down each side of this mountain in Glacier National Park in Montana. As the glaciers slid down the mountain, they ground its top into a long, thin point. Parts of this mountaintop are so thin that the sun shines through the rock.

▲ Long ago, a glacier dropped this huge boulder here.

◀ Spinning water dug this hole.

Everyday Science

Glaciers grind rock into dust. This dust is filled with **minerals** that help plants grow. Dust made by glaciers covers large parts of the midwestern United States. This dust makes the farmland very rich.

9

Water

Glaciers are not the only cause of erosion. The water in rivers also causes erosion. Every river, big or small, wears away the rock beneath it. Over time, rivers can carve steep-sided valleys. Rivers can cut mile-deep canyons into solid rock.

Some types of rock are softer than others. Sandstone and limestone are softer rocks. A river will wear away soft rock faster than hard rock.

In some rivers, the soft rock disappears, leaving a steep ledge of hard rock. The river water tumbles over the high ledge. It is a waterfall! Over time, the rushing water will wear away the hard rock, too. The waterfall will slowly creep backward as the hard rock wears away.

▲ **The Colorado River helped carve out this canyon.**

▲ Skogarfoss waterfall in Iceland

Horseshoe Falls is about 40,000 feet up the Niagara River from Lake Erie. The falls move backward at 5 feet per year. How long will it take for the waterfall to move all the way to Lake Erie?

The Grand Canyon

Water has formed some of the most beautiful places on Earth. The Grand Canyon was formed by water. It took five million years for the Colorado River to create the Grand Canyon. The river had to wear down through rock a mile thick.

THEY MADE A DIFFERENCE

John Wesley Powell made the Grand Canyon famous. In 1869, Powell convinced nine other men to join him on a trip down the Colorado River through the Grand Canyon. No one had ever made the trip before. No one had even tried.

Powell was a **geologist** (jee-OL-uh-jist) who learned much about the Grand Canyon during the trip. By the time the trip was over, he knew that the canyon had been eroded by the Colorado River.

Solve This

The Grand Canyon is the most famous canyon in the world, but it is not nearly the deepest. The Grand Canyon is about 5,000 feet deep. Cotahuasi Canyon in Peru is 11,000 feet deep. About how many times deeper is Cotahuasi than the Grand Canyon? Hint: Use estimation to find your answer.

◄ The amazing Grand Canyon stretches for 277 miles through northern Arizona. No wonder it took so long to create.

13

Snaking Rivers

Rivers change when they reach the bottom of a mountain. They are no longer rushing downhill. So they slow down. And as they flow across flat land, they get wider. These slow, wide rivers wear away more rock along their edges.

Rivers can also wind back and forth over flat ground. From the sky, these rivers look like snakes.

Where Rivers Dump Dirt

Have you ever looked at a river and thought it looked like it was full of dirt? Well, it probably was. Remember that rivers rush down mountains. As they go, they pick up lots of dirt and sand. Where does all the dirt and sand go? Most of the time, it is left at the spot where the river flows into the sea. The land made from the dirt and sand left behind by a river is called a **delta**.

▲ The Mara River in Africa winds back and forth.

The Badlands

There are no rivers in Badlands National Park in South Dakota. But water still plays an important role in erosion there. This time, the water is rain. Rain collects in ditches called **gullies**. The rainwater races down the gullies, cutting into the soft rock and exposing the colorful rock below.

▼ round, striped hills in Badlands National Park

▲ Many Egyptians still farm in the Nile Delta.

The Nile River runs through a desert. But dirt left by the Nile River has created rich soil in the Nile Delta. This soil has allowed people to farm there for thousands of years.

 POINT

Reread

Look again at the shapes that ice and water can make in the earth. What are some of the shapes made by glaciers? What are some of the shapes made by rivers?

Hazard Cave, ▶
Pickett State Park,
Tennessee

Everyday Science

As rainwater seeps into the earth, it gets into cracks in underground rock. The moving water eats away at the soft rock. Over time, these cracks grow wider until they become caves.

The dripping water in caves leaves behind minerals. These minerals build up into amazing shapes. Some look like curtains. Others look like lace. Many are very beautiful.

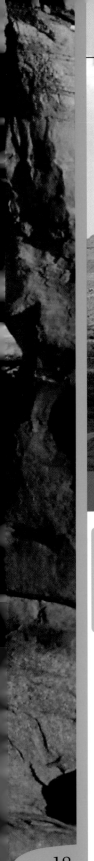

Wind

▲ **Monument Valley in Arizona**

Have you ever been at the beach on a windy day? As the wind whips down the beach, it picks up grains of sand. The wind stings your face because it's carrying these grains of sand.

Driven by the wind, these tiny bits of sand and dust can erode solid rock.

The sand in wind can carve interesting shapes in dry regions. Sometimes, whole cliffs have disappeared. All that remain are towers and arches looming over the dusty ground.

Careers in Science

People who study the Earth are called geologists. Some geologists study how Earth formed. Others predict how it will look in the future. Some geologists look for ways to stop erosion in places where it might hurt people. They work to stop farmland from washing away or houses from sliding down cliffs.

Shifting Dunes

In some deserts, the wind grinds all the loose rock down into sand. The sand collects in huge piles called **dunes**.

These dunes change shape all the time. The sand blows around, and the dunes shift and move. But if the sand is always blowing, how do dunes build up?

▼ The world's tallest sand dunes are in the Namib Desert in Africa. They rise as high as 1,300 feet.

For a dune to build up, it needs an anchor. An anchor is something that is rooted in one place in the sand. It might be a rock, a tree, or even a tiny bit of grass.

Some sand piles up next to the anchor, forming a mound. This mound becomes an anchor for even more sand. And so the dune grows larger.

▲ Sand is always on the move.

Blown Away

Wind can wear away rock. So why doesn't the wind also blow away all the dirt? The answer is plants. The roots of plants hold the soil in place. But what happens if the plants die?

In the 1930s, little rain fell across the central United States. Plants dried up and died. Almost no plants were left to hold the dirt in place. Wind blew the dirt across the fields and into the air. Between 1934 and 1938, the wind blew away three feet of soil from farms across Texas, Oklahoma, Kansas, and Colorado. The wind carried this dirt east all the way to the Atlantic Ocean. In May 1934, so much dirt filled the air in New York City that it was dark at noon. This time period is known as the Dust Bowl.

▲ The wind created dust storms that were like blizzards. People had to keep their doors and windows shut tight to keep out the dust.

DIGGING UP DINOS

The wind sometimes uncovers amazing things as it wears away rock. **Fossils** are animal bones that have turned into rock. The Gobi Desert in Asia is one of the best places to find dinosaur fossils. Every year, fierce desert winds blast away at the rocks, exposing more fossils. But, by a year later, the wind will have worn away those fossils, too—unless someone removes them.

Wind and Water Work Together

▲ These stacks of rocks are in Victoria, Australia.

Water cuts canyons through the mountains. Wind carves towers in the desert. And sometimes, wind and water work together. When waves pound against cliffs, they can crack the rock. More waves carry away the loose rock. At the same time, the wind is also wearing down the cliffs.

If waves erode all the way through the cliffs, an arch forms. Given enough time, the waves and wind will wear away the rock until the top of the arch falls into the water. This leaves a tower of rock standing alone in the water.

It's a Fact

Waves sometimes eat all the way through the top of a cave in a cliff, making a hole. This is called a **blowhole**. When waves smash into the cave, the water spouts up through the blowhole like a fountain.

Sandy Beaches

Did you know that all sand used to be part of bigger rocks? Rocks fall off cliffs into the ocean. The rocks are smashed and broken by waves. The pieces get tinier and tinier. Finally the pieces of rock are so tiny that we call them sand.

Waves carry sand along with them. The waves wash across the beach, leaving sand behind. Other waves pick up sand that is already on the beach and carry it back out to the ocean. Meanwhile, the wind blows the sand around. Beaches are always changing because of the wind and waves.

▼ Wind and waves constantly move the sand around.

It's a Fact

Beaches come in lots of colors. They can be yellow, brown, pink, black, or white. It all depends on what the sand is made of. Pink beaches are made of tiny bits of seashells. Black beaches are made from crushed **volcanic** rock and ash.

▲ This beach is on the island of Maui in Hawaii.

Disappearing Beaches

Most people love the beach. Some people love it so much that they build their houses right at the edge of the beach. But sometimes, the beach in front of their house disappears.

Many beaches disappear at a rate of three feet per year. After twenty years, an entire beach may be gone.

▲ The Pacific Ocean eroded the beach under these houses.

People try to stop beach erosion. Some put up seawalls. The walls are to keep waves from crashing on the beach and washing away the sand. Other people dump truckload after truckload of sand on the beach to replace the sand that has been washed away. But these methods seldom work. The wind and the waves are too powerful.

POINT

Make Connections

What are some ways that erosion helps people? What are some ways that erosion makes life more difficult for people?

▲ seawall in Havanna, Cuba

Conclusion

Earth may seem like it never changes. But it is changing all the time. Erosion plays a big part in these changes. Wind, water, and ice are constantly smashing rock and carrying it someplace new. They change the land.

The next time you're at the beach, watch the sand shift as waves crash along the shore. Go down to a river and look for crumbling dirt along the banks. No matter where you are, Earth is changing all around you. Nothing can stop the power of erosion.

Type of Erosion	Result
Glaciers	U-shaped valleys fjords potholes
Water	canyons caves deltas
Wind	sand dunes towering desert rocks
Wind and Water	sea caves rock arches beaches

Glossary

blowhole (BLOH-hohl) a hole in the top of a sea cave that seawater spurts through (page 25)

canyon (KAN-yuhn) a deep valley with high, steep sides (page 6)

delta (DEL-tuh) an area of land at the mouth of a river (page 14)

drumlin (DRUM-lin) an egg-shaped hill (page 9)

dune (DOON) a mound or ridge of sand that has been piled up by the wind (page 20)

erosion (i-ROH-zhuhn) wearing away by wind, water, or ice (page 2)

erratic boulder (i-RA-tik BOHL-duhr) a large rock carried by a glacier and left by itself far from where it started (page 9)

fjord (fee-AWRD) a steep-sided inlet of the sea carved by a glacier (page 7)

fossil (FOS-uhl) a bone or print of an ancient plant or animal (page 23)

geologist (jee-OL-uh-jist) a scientist who studies rocks or how Earth formed (page 13)

glacier (GLAY-shuhr) a large, slowly moving chuck of ice (page 4)

gully (GUH-lee) a ditch worn into the ground by running water (page 15)

mineral (MIN-uhr-uhl) a solid material found in nature that is not an animal or a plant (page 9)

volcanic (vol-KAN-ik) made by a volcano (page 27)

Solve This

Answers

1. Page 11   8,000 years
2. Page 13   2 times deeper

Index